DISCARD

Drinks
and
Desserts

ISBN 0-918831-32-6

U.S. Edition Copyright © 1985 by Gareth Stevens, Inc.

First published in South Africa by Daan Retief Publishers
Copyright © 1983.

U.S. Editor: Joseph F. Westphal
Cover Illustrations: Renée Graef
Typeset by Colony Pre-Press • Milwaukee, WI 53208 USA

Drinks and Desserts

S.J.A. de Villiers
and
Eunice van der Berg

Illustrated By
Marita Johnson

Gareth Stevens — Milwaukee

First Cookbook Library

Getting Ready To Cook
Drinks and Desserts
One Dish Meals
Vegetables and Salads
Breads and Biscuits
Cookies, Cakes and Candies

These books will show you how easy it is to cook and what fun it is, too.

Everything you have to do is clearly illustrated and the methods you will learn are the same as those used in advanced cookbooks. Once you learn these methods you will be able to follow recipes you find in any cookbook.

This book will teach you how to make drinks and desserts. We've included recipes for milk shakes and egg nog. You will also learn how to make desserts like pudding and custard.

If you are concerned about salt, sugar and fats in your diet, you may reduce the amount called for or substitute other ingredients in many of the recipes. Ask an adult for suggestions.

More information about nutrition, ingredients and cooking methods can be found in GETTING READY TO COOK, a companion volume to this book.

CONTENTS

Black arrows ➡ in some recipes are reminders to ask a grown-up to help you.

Banana Flip

(1 serving)

Take Out:

1 ice cream scooper
1 fork
1 mixing bowl
measuring cups
measuring spoons
egg beater
1 large glass, 1 teaspoon
1 saucer, 1 dinner plate

What You'll Need

1 ripe banana
1 teaspoon honey
5 teaspoons orange juice
⅔ cup milk
1 scoop ice cream

1. Peel the banana and mash it on the plate with the fork. Mix in the honey.

2. Put the banana mixture, orange juice and milk in the mixing bowl. Beat the mixture, using the egg beater until well blended.

3. Pour the mixture into the glass and scoop the ice cream on top.

4. Place the glass and teaspoon on the saucer.

Mixed Fruit Drink

(4 servings)

Take Out:

1 large pitcher
1 tablespoon
4 glasses

What You'll Need

32 ounces cranberry juice
1 cup apple juice
ice cubes
8 fresh mint leaves (optional)

1. Mix the cranberry juice and apple juice in the pitcher. Pour the mixture into four glasses.

2. Add an ice cube and two mint leaves to each glass and serve.

A mixture of pineapple and orange juice makes another delicious drink.

Eggnog

(1 serving)

Take Out:

1 small mixing bowl
egg beater
measuring spoons
measuring cups
sieve
1 glass

What You'll Need

1 egg
pinch of salt
2 teaspoons sugar
½ teaspoon vanilla extract
1 cup milk

1. Beat the egg well, using the egg beater and small mixing bowl.

2. Add the salt, sugar, vanilla, and milk and beat well again.

3. Pour the drink into the glass through the sieve and serve ice cold.

Take Out:

1 shaker with a tight lid
1 soup spoon
measuring cups
measuring spoons
1 large glass

What You'll Need

vanilla or chocolate ice cream
2 tablespoons chocolate syrup
½ cup cold milk

Chocolate Milk Shake

(1 serving)

1. Spoon five or six soup spoons of ice cream into the shaker. Add the chocolate syrup and milk. Stir.

2. Put the lid on the shaker and shake well until blended. You can use a blender instead.

3. Pour into the glass and serve immediately.

Iced Party Drink

(8 servings)

Take Out:

3 large pitchers
3 tablespoons
3 ice cube trays (empty)
8 glasses
1 paring knife
16 colored straws

What You'll Need

2 cups cranberry juice
2 cups lime-ade
2 cups orange juice
2 quarts lemonade

1. Mix each color cold drink in a separate pitcher. Follow the instructions on the cans.

2. Fill each ice cube tray with a different color cold drink in each.

3. Freeze for at least half a day. Remove from the freezer just before serving.

4. Place one or two cubes of each color ice in each glass. Fill the glasses with chilled lemonade.

5. Place a slice of lemon and two colored straws in each glass. Serve immediately.

English Tea For Two

Take Out:

electric tea kettle
measuring spoons
measuring cups
tea tray
2 cups, 2 saucers, 2 teaspoons
sugar bowl and sugar spoon
1 small milk pitcher
tea strainer
1 tea pot and towel
pitcher hot water

What You'll Need

tea leaves
boiling water
milk
sugar

1. Half fill the kettle with cold water and switch it on.

2. Arrange the tray as illustrated (no. 6 on this page). The handles of the cups and teapot point in the same direction. The teaspoons also point in that direction. The milk pitcher and sugar bowl should be full. Don't forget the tea strainer.

3. Rinse the teapot with a little boiling water.

4. Measure two teaspoons tea leaves into the hot teapot. Pour about two cups boiling water on the tea leaves.

5. Put the lid on and cover the teapot with the towel.

6. Place the pitcher filled with hot water on the tray next to the teapot.

7. Carry the tray to where the tea will be served.

8. Use the tea strainer to strain the tea into the cups. Offer your guest milk and sugar.

056050

Hints

Frost the edges of pudding glasses. Pour a little lemon juice into one saucer and sugar into another. Dip the edges of the pudding glasses firstly into the lemon juice, and then into the sugar. Allow to dry in the refrigerator before the fruit or pudding is served in the glasses.

Gelatin sets best in a refrigerator. It will not set faster in a freezer.

Sprinkle a little sugar over the custard so that a skin does not form on top. A round piece of butter paper placed directly on the custard will also prevent skin forming.

Desserts

Gelatin

(4 servings)

Take Out:

scissors
1 mixing bowl
wooden spoon
measuring cups
1 gelatin mold
or 4 individual dessert glasses

What You'll Need

1 package fruit flavored gelatin
1 cup boiling water
1 cup cold water

1. Cut open the package and shake the contents into the mixing bowl.

➡ 2. Pour the boiling water over the wooden spoon to dissolve all the gelatin crystals. Make sure that there are no crystals stuck to the wooden spoon or mixing bowl. Stir well.

3. Stir in the cold water.

4. Pour the gelatin into the mold or glasses and put it in the refrigerator to set.

Instant Pudding

(4 servings)

Take Out:

1 mixing bowl	measuring cups
scissors	tablespoon
egg beater	4 pudding glasses

What You'll Need

1 package instant pudding
cold milk

1. Read the instructions on the package to see how much milk you will need.

2. Measure the correct amount of milk in the measuring cup. Pour it into the mixing bowl.

3. Cut open the package of pudding and empty it over the milk in the mixing bowl.

4. Beat the mixture with the egg beater for the time indicted on the package.

5. Spoon the mixture into the glasses and let it set in the refrigerator.

Apple Brown Betty

(4 servings)

Take Out:

baking dish   measuring spoons
chopping board   small saucepan
paring knife   fork
measuring cups   oven mitts

What You'll Need

4 apples
½ cup sugar
⅓ cup butter or margarine
2 cups soft bread crumbs
¼ teaspoon cinnamon
½ cup hot water
1 tablespoon lemon juice

➡ 1. Preheat the oven to 350°. Grease the baking dish.

➡ 2. Quarter the apples on the chopping board with the paring knife. Remove the cores and peel the apples.

➡ 3. Cut each quarter into thin slices. Arrange these in the greased baking dish.

4. Sprinkle ¼ cup sugar on the apples.

➡ 5. Turn on the burner to low. Melt the butter or margarine in the saucepan.

6. Add the soft breadcrumbs, the remaining sugar, and the cinnamon to the butter. Blend well with the fork.

7. Spread the crumb mixture over the apples and level it with a fork.

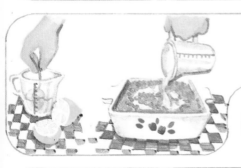

8. Mix the hot water and lemon juice and pour it evenly over the crumbs.

➡ 9. Bake it in the oven for 45 minutes. Remove it with the oven mitts. Turn off the oven heat.

10. Serve the Apple Brown Betty with custard or ice cream.

NOTE: Soft bread crumbs can be prepared in a blender or food processor in a few seconds. Ask an adult to help you.

Custard Sauce

(makes about 2 cups)

Take Out:

2 mixing bowls
measuring spoons
measuring cups
wooden spoon
egg beater

saucepan
teaspoon
plate
2 cup pitcher

What You'll Need

2 tablespoons cornstarch
3 tablespoons sugar
pinch of salt
4 tablespoons cold milk
2 cups hot milk
1 teaspoon vanilla extract
1 egg

1. Blend the cornstarch, sugar, and salt in one mixing bowl. Stir in the cold milk with the wooden spoon until smooth.

2. Whisk the egg in the other mixing bowl for one minute. Rest the egg beater on the plate until needed again.

➡ 3. Turn the burner to a medium heat. Boil the milk in the saucepan. Reduce the heat to low as soon as the milk starts boiling.

➡ 4. Pour a little hot milk into the cornstarch mixture and stir well.

➡ 5. Add the remaining hot milk to the saucepan. Add the cornstarch mixture, stirring all the time with the wooden spoon.

➡ 6. Stir the custard sauce continuously until it boils again. Let it boil slowly for three minutes. Continue stirring.

➡ 7. Remove the saucepan from the heat. Have someone ready to help you with the next step.

➡ 8. Beat the egg again with the egg beater while the other person pours the boiling mixture slowly onto the egg.

9. Add the vanilla and beat again to blend.

➡ 10. Pour the custard sauce back into the saucepan and stir it over a low heat until it starts to boil again. Remove from the stove immediately.

➡ 11. Turn off the burner. Stir the custard sauce for a while after you have removed it from the stove.

12. Allow the custard sauce to cool. Pour it into the pitcher.

13. Serve the sauce on cake or pudding.

Banana Custard

(4 servings)

Take Out:

pudding bowl
knife
tablespoon
teaspoon
measuring cups

What You'll Need

2 cups custard sauce
4 ripe bananas
¼ cup apricot jam
2 tablespoons chopped nuts
(pecan or walnuts)

1. Prepare a custard sauce (page 22). Leave to cool completely. Pour it into the pudding bowl.

2. Peel and slice the bananas. Stir into the custard sauce.

3. Dot the apricot jam on the custard using the teaspoon.

4. Sprinkle the chopped nuts on top of the Banana Custard.

Dessert Mountain

(6 servings)

Take Out:

chopping board
knife
pudding bowl
2 spoons
small mixing bowl
egg beater
fork

What You'll Need

firm red gelatin (prepared
  beforehand; see page 16)
2 cups custard sauce (see page 22)
6 slices sponge cake
⅓ cup smooth apricot jam
½ cup orange juice
½ cup light cream

1. Cut the sponge cake and spread the slices with apricot jam.

2. Arrange the slices in the pudding bowl.

3. Sprinkle the cake with the orange juice, using the spoon.

4. Pour the custard sauce evenly over the damp sponge cake and leave for 30 minutes.

5. Use a fork to break up the firm gelatin in the bowl in which it has set.

6. Arrange a ring of red gelatin on top of the custard in the pudding bowl.

7. Use the egg beater to whip the cream in the small mixing bowl taking care not to whip for too long. The whipped cream should just be firm enough to stick to the egg beater.

8. Spoon the whipped cream in the middle of the gelatin ring on top of the custard sauce.

Orange Pudding

(6 servings)

Take Out:

grater, small plate   large mixing bowl
knife, fork   measuring cups, tea cup
orange juicer   egg beater
small mixing bowl   tablespoon, teaspoon

What You'll Need

2 cups orange juice
1 orange
2 tablespoons gelatin
¼ cup cold water
½ cup boiling hot water
3 eggs
¾ cups sugar

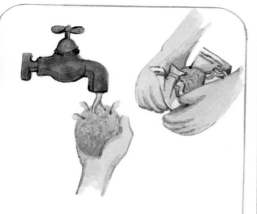

1. Wash the orange in cold water and wipe dry.

2. Grate the outer rind of the orange on the finest grid of the grater. Remove the grated rind from the grater with the fork. You should have about one tea-spoon grated rind.

3. Squeeze out the orange juice and pour it into the measuring cup. Add more orange juice until you have two cups.

4. Measure ¼ cup cold water into the tea cup. Sprinkle the gelatin powder on the cold water so that all of it gets wet. Leave for five minutes until it thickens.

5. Pour ½ cup boiling water on the gelatin and stir it with a tea-spoon. It will become clear when the gelatin has dissolved.

6. Separate the eggs carefully. Drop the egg whites into the small mixing bowl and the yolks into the large mixing bowl.

7. Whisk the egg yolks with the egg beater. Whisk in the sugar one spoonful at a time. The mixture will become creamy and light.

8. Add the gelatin, orange rind and orange juice. Stir with the tablespoon.

9. Leave the mixture in the refrigerator until it starts to set. Draw a spoon through the pudding to make sure it is partly set.

10. Wash the egg beater and dry it thoroughly. Whisk the egg whites until a stiff white foam clings to the egg beater. Do not whisk any longer.

11. Fold the stiff egg whites carefully into the thick orange pudding using the tablespoon. Do not stir.

12. Pour the orange dessert into the pudding bowl and allow it to set properly in the refrigerator. Serve it with whipped cream.

INDEX

Black arrows ➡ in some recipes are reminders to ask a grown-up to help you.